IMAGES OF
England

NORTH TELFORD
WELLINGTON, OAKENGATES
AND SURROUNDING AREAS

A family snapshot taken in the back garden in Donnington Wood in the 1920s or 1930s. In the background can be seen a beam engine and pit head gear at a nearby coal mine, typical of the area.

IMAGES OF
England

NORTH TELFORD
WELLINGTON, OAKENGATES
AND SURROUNDING AREAS

John Powell & Michael A. Vanns

TEMPUS

First published 1995
Reprinted 2000, 2004

Tempus Publishing Limited
The Mill, Brimscombe Port,
Stroud, Gloucestershire, GL5 2QG
www.tempus-publishing.com

British Library Cataloguing in Publication Data.
A catalogue record for this book is available from the British Library.

ISBN 0 7524 0124 6

Typesetting and origination by Tempus Publishing Limited.
Printed in Great Britain.

Donnington Wood Girls School Class 3 around the turn of the century.

Contents

The Lilleshall Company's Lodge Furnaces at Donnington Wood, being demolished in about 1890. Remains of the bases can now be seen in Granville Country Park.

The Wrekin is still the most prominent and permanent landmark in north Telford, and in this view only the tractor dates the scene to 1957.

Introduction

The aim of this volume is to provide a glimpse of North Telford's past by means of historic photographs. The pictures are not restricted to the changes wrought by Telford New Town over the past quarter of a century, which have indeed been quite dramatic, but date back over a hundred years, during which time things have been constantly altering, albeit at a steadier rate.

It is hoped that the book may appeal equally to those who have come to live or work in the town in recent times, and to those who may remember with mixed emotions the people and places which existed before the New Town came along.

The photographs have been drawn almost exclusively from the collection built up by the Library of the Ironbridge Gorge Museum Trust over the past 25 years, and the Museum would like to place on record its thanks to those many generous local people who have either donated photographs or allowed them to be copied.

The compilers of the book have been responsible for the storage, conservation and indexing of this collection for 15 years, and the selection is very much a personal one. An attempt has been made to balance photographs of places with those showing human interest. Some of the images will have been seen in other local books but, since these are mostly out of print, this has not been seen as a reason for excluding them. Many others are published for the first time, including a number taken in the 1950s and 1960s by the late W. Howard Williams, a pioneer local industrial historian who donated his negatives to the Museum many years ago.

The area covered is largely that which was excluded from the original Dawley New Town – ie settlements north of the Holyhead Road which were incorporated later on when the designated area and target population were expanded. This includes Wellington, Oakengates, St Georges, Hadley, Trench, Wrockwardine Wood and Donnington. Ketley and the Town Centre have also been added to this volume. A companion book is available covering the rest of South Telford.

Space precludes lengthy captions, and those wanting to learn more about the area are referred to the *Victoria County History of Shropshire* Volume XI covering Telford, Barrie Trinder's excellent *Industrial Revolution in Shropshire* and, for the more recent changes, to *Telford, the making of Shropshire's New Town* by Maurice de Soissons.

Anyone having old photographs of their own is urged to deposit copies with a local museum, library or record office. All too often, their relevance goes unrecognised if the owner dies or moves away and, as it is hoped this volume may demonstrate, they prove a marvellous resource if made available to the general public.

John Powell
Coalbrookdale, May 1995

Wellington looking due south on 28 May 1958 with the ground to the left of the Methodist Chapel cleared ready for the extension of Victoria Street to form the new ring road.

One
Wellington

New Street, Wellington, probably photographed in the late 1920s looking towards the town centre. Unlike in Victorian street scenes, no one is conscious of the camera, the novelty of photography having worn off.

Corbett's ironmonger's shop in Church Street, Wellington. Items on display outside include a meat safe, a garden seat and a ladder. In the shop window there is a bird cage for sale, whilst copper kettles can be seen in the window above. The photograph is dated 1 September 1894.

Although individual buildings and shops have changed since this view was taken in the early 1900s, Market Street and Church Street, Wellington, are still recognisable today.

Agricultural machinery produced by S. Corbett & Son of Wellington, together with six employees, photographed at a show at Bridgnorth in the 1890s. Certificates pinned up reveal that several prizes have been won. The portable engine in the foreground allowed working demonstrations to be given to potential customers.

The centre of Wellington with the market hall prominent in the middle of this mid-1970s aerial photograph. The open space to the left of the hall was the site of the Wrekin Brewery.

Looking east along New Street, Wellington, in the early 1900s. The dog has obviously found something interesting in the doorway of the shoe shop.

Even before today's restricted vehicular access to the centre of Wellington, people still walked confidently down the middle of the road as is obvious in this late 1890s view.

Interior of Wellington Market, 31 July 1975.

McClure's ladies' outfitter's shop between Duke Street and Crown Street, Wellington in the mid 1950s.

Interior view of McClure's shop taken on the same day as the picture above. An advertisement for the 'Little X' girdle appears bottom right.

The west side of Market Square, Wellington, in the 1970s with Hobsons printers still in business.

Inside Hobsons Printing Works, Wellington, a photograph taken not as you might think in 1900, but a generation later in 1975.

Wellington from the air on 22 November 1981 with the former London & North Western and Great Western Joint Railway opened at the end of 1849 sweeping in from Shrewsbury. To the right in the centre of the photograph the cattle market and adjacent railway goods yard can be seen, now the site of Morrisons superstore and carpark.

Ex-Great Western Railway, 'Criccieth Castle' no. 5026, seen entering Wellington station from Shrewsbury with the 11.02am departure for London Paddington on 24 June 1961. Wellington was the principal main line station until Telford Central opened on 12 May 1986. Today it is not possible to travel directly to London without changing trains at Wolverhampton or Birmingham.

Church Street, Wellington, a few years after the Second World War, apart from the cars and lorries, virtually unchanged since the photograph at the top of page 13 was taken, with the trees in front of All Saints enhancing the scene.

A busy 1920s scene in the Market Square, Wellington. Notice the man in white overalls balanced on a plank supported between two ladders on the right. Is he painting the frontage or about to mend the shop awning?

Morris commercial van used by Wellington Laundry for collections and deliveries around the town in the early 1950s.

Wellington library was brand new when this photograph was taken in the opening years of the twentieth century, and fortunately the building still looks like this today, only the houses to the left having been demolished to make way for a modern extension. For a brief period, the celebrated poet, Philip Larkin, worked in the library.

Samuel Tinsley's shop at 61 High Street, Wellington, in the 1920s. A local performance of *Puss in Boots* is being advertised in the right-hand window.

Wellington on a sunny summer day in the early 1980s. This view shows very clearly how the railway isolated All Saints Church from the town centre in the late 1840s.

In the 1960s many towns and cities demolished substantial Victorian buildings like this because they were considered outdated. Here, in November 1961, Barclays Bank on the corner of Queen Street, Wellington, comes down to make way for a more modern structure.

Looking south east on 24 November 1973 along the truncated High Street, Wellington, as work progresses on the new pedestrian path under Victoria Street.

New Street, Wellington, thirty years ago. It is interesting to contrast this scene with that at the bottom of page 12, noticing how the buildings in the centre of that view had by the 1960s been replaced by Waterworths Food Market.

A rather posed photograph of the Hiatt Ladies' College. All the skipping ropes on the left are in the air at the same time! Under the canopy, a needlework class is at work in the open air.

The firm of G.H. York of New Street, Wellington, seen in the process of sinking a borehole to augment the town's water supply in the 1930s.

Show staged by the staff for inmates at Wellington Poor Law Institution, later the Wrekin Hospital, in the 1920s. Nurse Gladys Shepherd is in the centre in the front row. Mr and Mrs Chapman were 'Master' and 'Matron' of the Institution at this time.

Guides from the 1st Wellington Girl Guide troop at camp at Stokesay Court in the 1920s.

Before traffic lights, this is what the Cock Hotel road junction, Wellington, looked like on a snowy night in 1956.

Wellington once had several maltings. This one in Haygate Road survived until the early 1960s, though the date when it was last used is not known.

GENERAL VIEW OF THE SHROPSHIRE BREWERY, WELLINGTON.

The Shropshire Brewery was situated on the Holyhead Road, just west of the Cock Hotel. This engraving from Barnard's *Noted Breweries of Great Britain and Ireland* published in 1889 was probably drawn from a photograph.

The chimney of the Wrekin Brewery, on the south side of Market Street, Wellington, being felled on 15 January 1975. It was the town's last brewery, and had closed in 1969.

Looking from Wellington railway station at the buildings shortly to be demolished to make way for the current John Menzies shop. Unfortunately this *Wellington Journal* photograph is not dated, but if DAW 721C is new, then it's *c.* 1964.

'Brown paper packages tied up with string'. Packing and dispatching the *Wellington Journal* in October 1957.

'Hot metal'. The *Wellington Journal*'s linotype machines in 1957, long before the computer revolution fundamentally changed journalism.

Bennett's Bank, Wellington, looking east in the early 1950s. A British Railways lorry emerges from the Hadley direction, whilst a Corona delivery heads up Arleston Lane. There are now traffic lights here adjacent to the 'Bucks Head'.

Wellington Special Constables who served during the 1939–1945 war. The tower of St Patrick's Roman Catholic Church is in the background.

Looking north along King Street, Wellington towards the now demolished Baptist Chapel. The date of the photograph is not known, but the price of petrol reveals it is before the Middle East crisis of the 1970s.

Wellington College seen from the golf course in the first decade of the twentieth century.

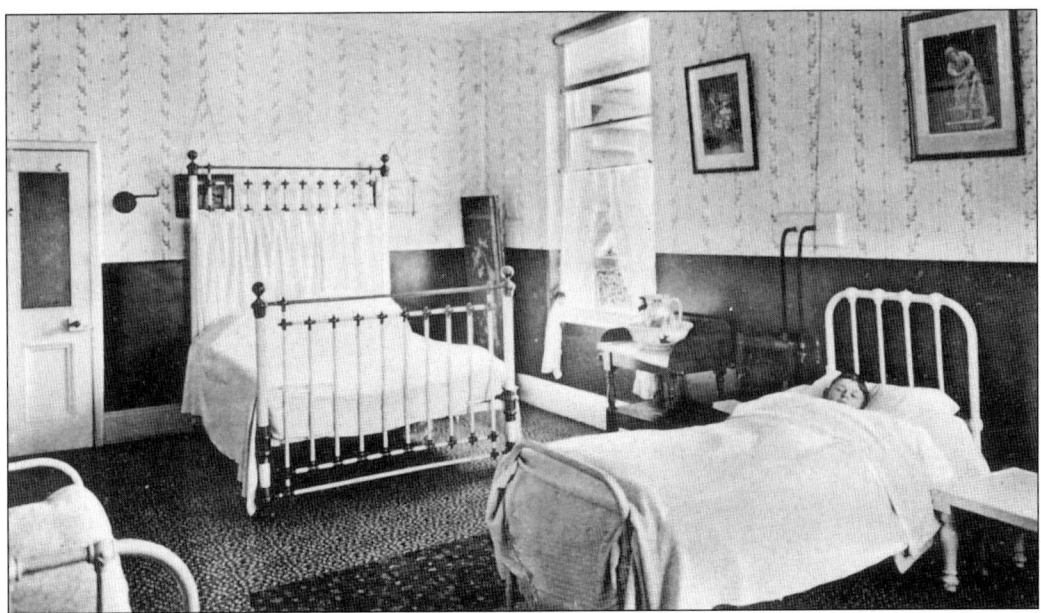

For those fortunate enough to attend Wellington College before the First World War, even being sick had its privileges.

Church Street, Wellington. No special occasion; no one posed for the camera; just an ordinary day in the 1920s.

At the beginning of the twentieth century, E.J. Capsey ran his general drapers, milliners and outfitters business from this shop at 15 Market Square, Wellington.

The solid late nineteenth century architecture of Wellington's Hiatt Ladies' College from where solid late nineteenth century citizens were produced.

Concentration. High walls prevented prying eyes from looking in, and wandering minds from gazing out.

Wellington Town Football Club 1920/21 season. Formed in 1899, they changed their name to Telford United in 1969.

Motorists leaving Wellington in the direction of Shrewsbury may catch sight of the truncated tower of Cluddley Mill towards the Wrekin. This photograph was taken before its conversion into a house a few years ago.

Two

Oakengates

'Number, please?' Operators at work in Oakengates Telephone Exchange on 11 October 1961.

Market Street, Oakengates about a century ago, looking towards the Albion Mound. One of the shops on the left advertises itself as a 'fish and chipped potatoes restaurant'. Postcard published by L.W. Marshall, whose shop can be seen on the right. They also had a shop in nearby Oxford Street.

A Midland Red bus bound for Wellington waits to proceed from Lion Street into Market Street and under the railway. Until 1978, a number of independent firms such as Brown's and Martlew's also operated in the area under the auspices of the Shropshire Omnibus Association.

Grocer's shop at 4 Market Street, Oakengates early this century. A notice advertising 'Ices' is wedged in amongst the bananas.

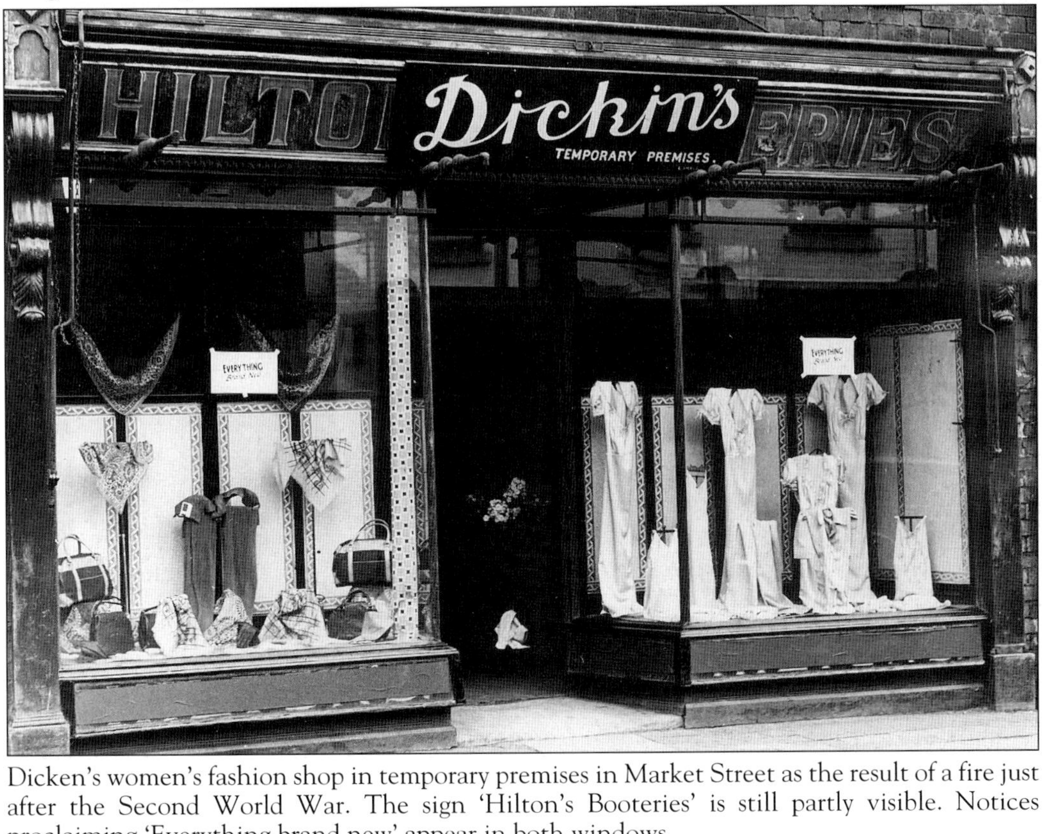

Dicken's women's fashion shop in temporary premises in Market Street as the result of a fire just after the Second World War. The sign 'Hilton's Booteries' is still partly visible. Notices proclaiming 'Everything brand new' appear in both windows.

Looking down Market Street towards the railway bridge between the wars. Few of the buildings seen here are recognisable today.

Arthur Scott Kitching's chemist's shop in Market Street, Oakengates, photographed before 1917, with the entrance to Arthur Ward's dental surgery to the left. The left hand window contains watches and pipes, whilst advertisements for 'Death Trap' fly paper are prominent on the right.

Oakengates Carnival procession heads down Market Street on 4 June 1966.

A curiously de-populated Market Street in the 1970s. The plaque at the top of the building on the right reads 'Oakengates Market 1826. Rebuilt 1869'.

Market Street, Oakengates at the beginning of the motor age – note the early 'Pratt's' petrol pump on the left. Shoes on offer at Olivers vary in price from 3/6d (17½p) to 8/11d (44p) per pair.

Late nineteenth century view of the east end of Market Street, Oakengates, looking up Station Hill. The railway station was the second one to be provided in Oakengates, and was on the line from Wellington to Coalport.

Oakengates Station seen from the bottom of Station Hill. The line was closed in the 1960s, and the elevated section of the Queensway road has taken its place dominating this part of the town.

Looking down Oxford Street, Oakengates towards Market Street a hundred years ago. The building at the far end survives, though the Post Office has now moved to the other side of the road. Postcard published by Marshalls, whose shop can be seen on the right.

Pouring metal at Maddock's Foundry in Oakengates on 16 October 1979. Since then, the works has closed, the site has been cleared, and new houses are beginning to appear.

The goods yard at Oakengates station on the branch to Coalport. All this has now disappeared with the exception of the goods shed with the long slope to the roof, which survives as a tile warehouse in the shadow of the elevated Queensway.

John Maddock's Foundry is prominent in this 1930s view looking north east towards Canongate, Oakengates. The route of the Wellington to Coalport railway line, seen in the background, is now followed by the Queensway at this point. The station on the main line to Birmingham is visible in the foreground.

Having stopped at Wellington, a Birkenhead to London Paddington express accelerates through Oakengates station towards the tunnel, next stop Wolverhampton Low Level in the early 1960s. The locomotive is Castle class no. 7015 *Carn Brea Castle*.

A well-known feature of Oakengates until just a few years ago was the former Wesleyan chapel incorporated into Maddock's works near the station.

The Walker Institute, Hartsbridge Road, Oakengates, built in 1926. View looking south west, with the Holyhead Road top left and Hartshill Road bottom right.

Billy Lloyd's cobbler's shop in Bridge Street, Oakengates. It was later dismantled and re-erected at Blists Hill Open Air Museum complete with all its contents.

A general view towards Oakengates thirty years ago, looking down Dukes Hill, Ketley Bank. The wooded Cockshutt Piece is prominent on the horizon.

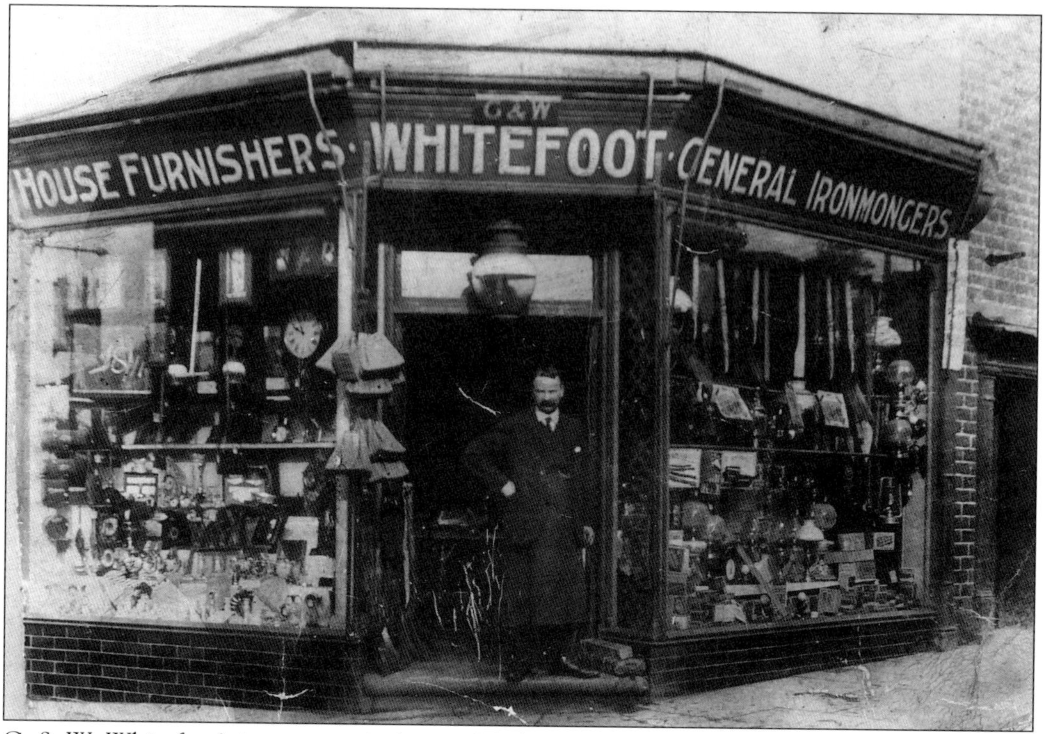

G. & W. Whitefoot's ironmonger's shop in Market Street, Oakengates early this century.

Two Oakengates women out for a spin in a Wolseley car between the wars.

Mumpton Hill Cottages, Oakengates, the scene of a gruesome murder in July 1910 when a man killed his wife and then committed suicide with the same razor. 'X' marks the spot.

Oakengates Brass Band around 1910. On the table is a trophy they have won, made by the Coalport China Company.

The Brown Lion Inn, Lion Street, Oakengates, 1960.

A tranquil view looking along New Street, Oakengates towards Wombridge a few years later. Now part of the Oakengates one way system.

These premises in Slaney Street, marked on the Ordnance Survey maps of the 1880s as an iron foundry, are little altered since this picture of 30 years ago, though the chimney is now reduced to a stump.

Oakengates embraces 1960s architecture. Houses on Slaney Street are visible in the background.

Owen's cycle shop at the top of Market Street, Oakengates before the First World War. Five members of the Owen family are in the car, whilst Joseph Herrington looks on from the shop doorway. Owen's survives, but now deals in electrical goods rather than bicycles.

Market Street, Oakengates last century, looking towards the railway bridge from the vantage point similar to the picture on page 36. A horse and cart emerges from Oxford Street on the left.

Three
St Georges & Snedshill

A group photograph taken on the occasion of the wedding of Tom Ashley to Pollie Addison at St Georges in 1906. A superb array of headgear can be seen.

The new St Georges Institute, just west of the church, which was erected in 1899 on land donated by the 4th Duke of Sutherland. A handsome building, incorporating bright red terracotta, it unfortunately stands disused at the time of writing.

A crowd has gathered to watch the Victorian photographer take this picture looking east along West Street, St Georges, with Church Street beyond. Stafford Street comes in to the right of the lamp-post and Gower Street goes off to the left.

In this later picture, the photographer stands at the crossroads in St Georges – now a mini-roundabout – and points the camera due south down Stafford Street. The attractive corner block with the curved frontage on the left is the most distinctive feature of the centre of St Georges.

Doctor Davies, who had a practice in the Square, St Georges in the 1920s, seen on his Velocette motorcycle. Always compassionate to the poor, who numbered more than a few amongst his patients, he would allow them to pay by installments or accept vegetables in lieu of cash.

Snedshill Brickworks looking west four decades ago, with the Holyhead Road to Ketley and Wellington clearly visible top centre. The road from the Greyhound down to Oakengates leads off to the right, and the road to Ketley Bank can also be seen top left.

Snedshill Brickworks looking north west across Oakengates towards Wombridge and Trench. The few distinctive chimneys which survive, marked 'L Co' on the side, can be glimpsed from the Holyhead Road, seen in the picture, and from Queensway which now cuts through the hillside to the left before skirting round the east of Oakengates.

Another 1950s view showing the chimneys of Snedshill Brickworks in the foreground with the Priorslee Furnaces in the middle distance on the left. Stirchley Chimney is in the distance. The area in between is now totally transformed by the building of Telford Town Centre.

Members of Snedshill Mission Hall who served tea at the Methodist rally held there in 1901. No fewer than seven members of the Rushton family appear in the group.

The church in St Georges, formerly known as Pain's Lane, was consecrated in 1862. This postcard was issued before the tower was completed in 1929. Situated on the top of a ridge, the tower with a pyramidical roof forms something of a landmark from the lower lying areas to the north east.

Children from St Georges' Infants School, 1926.

Different collar styles are visible in this group portrait of boys from St Georges' School dated 1912.

Derelict buildings at the south end of Gower Street, St Georges in January 1973. The shop front was later removed to Blists Hill Open Air Museum, where it forms the front of a printers shop.

In the 1880s, Snedshill Forge was thought prestigious enough to feature in a textbook on the economics of the iron industry. This illustration from the book shows a puddler checking the state of the iron in a puddling furnace for making wrought iron.

Once removed from the puddling furnace and hammered flat, the wrought iron would be passed back and forth through these rolls to form boiler plate. The workforce pose for the photograph without any hot iron visible.

Workers from Snedshill on a works outing at an unknown destination in the 1930s. It was obviously a fine day, as the charabanc on the left has the canvas roof rolled back.

Harry Edwards (left) and a group of striking miners at their own pit at The Nabb in 1912. Notice the upturned bicycle being used to wind coal from the shaft.

A mission church was built at The Nabb in 1884 on land given by the Lilleshall Company. It was enlarged in 1892 to accommodate a congregation of 170. Today the church, which latterly only saw occasional use, has gone, but a notice on a nearby tree still proclaims that it is Lilleshall Company property.

A similar corrugated iron mission church built in 1888 near Granville Colliery, was closed during the Second World War. Here a new congregation is seen celebrating its re-opening in March 1957. Attendances like this were not maintained, however, and in the late 1970s after another period of disuse, the chapel was dismantled and re-erected at Blists Hill Open Air Museum.

Four
The Lilleshall Influence

The Lilleshall Company's testing department. In order to maintain the quality of its iron, which was some of the best in the country, samples were regularly tested by drilling, twisting, bending and shearing.

A group of Lilleshall Company workers pose alongside a hydraulic ram at the foot of the Priorslee Furnaces *c*. 1900.

Looking south across the Lilleshall Company's Priorslee Furnaces in 1958. The junction of Furnace Road and Church Road with Holyhead Road can be seen in the foreground, with St Peter's Church, Priorslee on the left. The Shrewsbury to Birmingham railway is just visible beyond the works complex paralleled by the now disappeared Wellington to Coalport line.

The beam blowing engines 'David and Sampson' which provided the blast for the furnaces at Priorslee. Retained latterly only as standby engines in case of breakdown, they were dismantled and re-erected at Blists Hill Open Air Museum in the early 1970s.

The physical strength needed to work in a rolling mill is apparent from this photograph of some of the men from Snedshill Forge in 1900. '9 Mill Snedshill' has been hastily chalked on a piece of wood prior to the photograph being taken.

Priorslee Furnaces made a spectacular sight at night, as this photograph taken in June 1937 from a nearby road demonstrates. Beyond the railway wagons can be seen all the boilers needed to keep the plant supplied with steam 24 hours a day.

The vast scale of the Priorslee complex is apparent from this post war view looking north west, with Snedshill Brickworks beyond. The Holyhead Road passes right to left in the background, with Priorslee Church just to the north.

The massiveness of Priorslee Furnaces, as seen in this 1930s photograph, was later obscured by the construction of other buildings in front of them. Behind can be seen a hoist for lifting up the raw materials to feed the furnaces, which are connected by a high level walkway.

Engines constructed by the Lilleshall Company for Shanghai Waterworks in China, seen inside their works at the New Yard in 1927.

Though the manufacture of iron at Priorslee ceased in 1959, rolling and re-rolling continued into the early 1980s. A strip of red hot iron is being manoeuvred through the rolls in this photograph taken in June 1975.

What could be better than this after a hard day's physical work? A view taken inside the Lilleshall Company's employees' washroom in 1950.

From the 1860s, the Lilleshall Company's engineering activities were concentrated at the New Yard in Gower Street, St Georges. This view is taken from the back of the complex, looking north eastwards towards Donnington Wood. This scene is being increasingly transformed as new building takes place to the east: the works survives as small industrial units.

The sheer scale of some of the construction work undertaken by the company can be seen in this 1902 view of a twin winding engine for a coal mine.

Engineer-in-charge Richard Frith, poses alongside a huge crushing and pulverising plant inside the New Yard in about 1914.

Some of the Lilleshall Company's prestigious contracts involved trips abroad. Richard Frith, seen in the previous photograph but now in shirt-sleeves order, poses with Reece Barker in Bombay, India, where they had gone to install some pumping engines in 1913.

An extensive railway network connected the various Lilleshall Company works and mines. The top cast iron notice reads: 'Trespassing on the Private Railways of the Lilleshall Company Limited is hereby prohibited. Should any employee or person trespass in defiance of this notice they will do so at their own risk and peril and the company will not be responsible in case of any accident or injury to such trespasser. By order, T.E. Freeston, Managing Director'.

Two of the company's locomotives were in attendance during the demolition of a concrete bunker at Priorslee in 1936. No.5, on the right, had been purchased from the Great Western Railway, the other loco, probably no. 10, purchased from Peckett's of Bristol in 1901.

Two shunters and driver pose with Lilleshall Company locomotive no .4 *Constance*. This engine was built at the company's own works in 1865 and scrapped in 1957.

Locomotives nos. 6 and 11, and a company owned railway wagon at Hollinswood Sidings in the 1930s, with the chimneys of Priorslee visible beyond. The entire railway system closed in 1959, with many staff enjoying a last run standing in open trucks shortly before closure.

The scene at the bottom of the furnace on the occasion of the last cast of iron at Priorslee Furnaces, 27 March 1959.

The pig-bed at Priorslee Furnaces on the same day.

Demolition of the blowing-engine house at Priorslee in the early 1970s. The beams from engines 'David and Sampson' are being removed for re-erection at Blists Hill Open Air Museum.

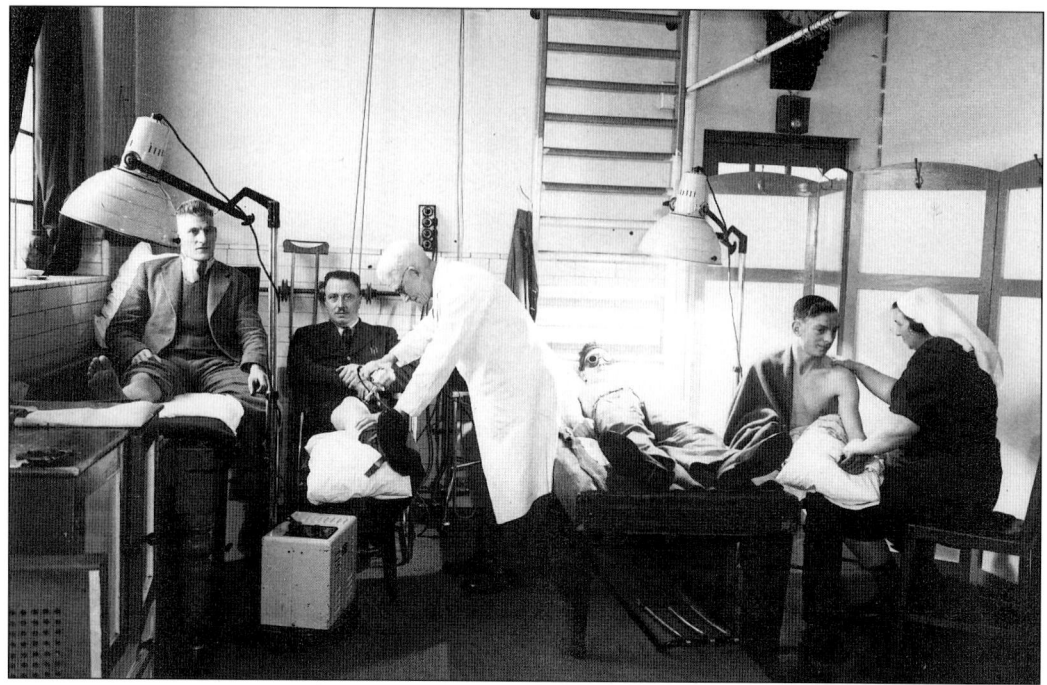

Though obviously posed, this photograph from 1950 shows that the Lilleshall Company took the welfare of its employees seriously. Ben Evans (in the white coat) and Nurse E. Hobson, attend to aches and pains in the company's Massage Department.

Thirty-eight employees of the Lilleshall Company line up for presentation of a silver tankard each in recognition of over 50 years' service to the company. In 1950, the firm had over 80 employees who had reached this landmark.

Five

Ketley, Hadley, and Trench

Distinctive guillotine lock gates, designed by Thomas Telford, were a feature of the Trench Branch of the Shrewsbury Canal. This shows the one at Hadley Park Lock thirty years ago, before the tranquillity of the area was disturbed by the building of the Queensway road just to the north, and the encroachment of new factories.

Ivy Colliery at Clares Lane, Ketley in 1934. This small mine operated for a short period of time in the 1920s and 1930s employing only about a dozen men. The mine owner, Edward Harris, is the man in the centre wearing a suit.

The south elevation of Bank House, Ketley, a view now becoming increasingly obscured by the growth of trees. At one time the house was occupied by the ironmaster Richard Reynolds, and later by his son William, when it was relatively secluded in extensive grounds. It is now surrounded by houses, and the busy Mossey Green Way passes behind it to the west.

Children, and a man using an umbrella to shield himself from the sun pose on the Holyhead Road where the Wellington to Much Wenlock and Craven Arms railway crossed the road at a level crossing. View looking east with Ketley station and signalbox to the south of the road about a century ago.

Ketley station from the south west in the 1960s. One mixed train, conveying passengers and goods, departed from here towards Wenlock on Saturday mornings, the passengers being mainly men from the local ironworks. Although the line has gone, the building survives as a private house.

Looking south across the Holyhead Road between Ketley and Oakengates in 1958 towards Red Lake Church. Part of Castle View is under construction. The canal once crossed the road in front of the white buildings which, until recently, were in use as a discount furniture warehouse.

This very smart Super-Sentinel was purchased by the Sinclair Iron Company of Ketley in October 1926, though they only kept it for seven years before selling it on to an operator in Liverpool Docks.

Inside the Sinclair Ironworks in Ketley, a generation ago. Originally set up by Duncan Sinclair following an argument with the Coalbrookdale Company, it was ironic that both concerns were later absorbed into the Allied Ironfounders Group and now find themselves together as part of Glynwed.

Seldom seen from the road, Ketley Hall was a residence for local ironmasters until late last century. Just south west of the Hall is the site of the country's first canal inclined plane, built by William Reynolds. A road nearby is named 'The Incline'.

Hadley High Street *c.* 1910. Two boys and a girl pose for the photographer by the gas lamp on the right. There were once some elegant houses here, as shown on page 79.

Hadley Junction, just south of the Castle Works, where the Wellington to Coalport railway line (right) branched off the line from Wellington to Stafford via Newport. Passenger traffic on both lines ceased more than thirty years ago.

The Horse Shoes, Ketley. Photograph specially taken for a calendar of pub views distributed by the Wrekin Brewery in 1958.

Woman standing at a gate in Hadley High Street early this century. The house has some fine architectural details, in addition to cast`iron fencing and gates.

The castellated tower of Hadley Park windmill is the 'castle' from which the nearby Castle Works derived its name. Once a rural backwater disturbed only by the passing of canal boats, this area is now surrounded by new roads and modern factories.

The main entrance and offices of the Castle Car Works, Hadley, looking north east. This photograph was probably taken between 1900–1904, when G.F. Milnes & Co. of Birkenhead were manufacturing tramcars on the site.

Looking south west towards Wellington from Hadley ninety years ago. A signpost on the left points to Shawbirch and Wem. In the distance is the 'Old Cross Keys' with the Wrekin visible beyond.

The Castle Car Works, Hadley, looking south west towards the Wrekin. Though showing the works when occupied by Milnes of Birkenhead (trams can been seen in the yard), the picture was used by Sankeys in their publicity literature. Notice the basin and locks on the Shrewsbury Canal to the right.

Sankey Patent Pressed Steel Wheels
fitted with Warland Detachable Rims

A—Loose Flange.	C—Valve Hood.	F—Slots for use in	H—Fixed lip of wheel.
B—Bolts and Nuts for holding flange A.	D—Removable Rim.	contracting rim.	J —Bolt holes of flange.
	E—Gap Piece.	G—Rim of Wheel.	K—Valve hole.

PRICE LIST OF SANKEY-WARLAND WHEELS.

Size of Tyre.	Price of Four Sankey-Warland Wheels, with one spare rim and the necessary tools (*No hubs included*).	Code Word.
800 × 85 810 × 90 810 × 100 815 × 105 820 × 120	£34 0 0	Spianano
880 × 120 895 × 135	£35 0 0	Spianasse

Extra Rim and Fittings - **38/-**   Bag of Tools, complete - **26/-**

WHEN ORDERING,

Send—1. Sketches giving full external details of hubs including number, position, and diameter of bolts, *or*
2. One front and one rear hub from the chassis, preferably with the wheels, *or*
3. Makers' name, H.P., year of manufacture and number of chassis, when we will, if possible, obtain drawings from the manufacturers.

Subject to our general Conditions of Sale.

Above prices are without engagement, and all goods will be invoiced at the price ruling at time of despatch.

Sankey products as shown in a company catalogue dating from 1924. For some reason, all wheels made were fully guaranteed by the manufacturer unless fitted to cars used for hire.

Joseph Sankey's Hadley Castle Works, looking south east about 40 years ago. The Wellington–Newport railway passes from right to left beyond the works, with the branch to Coalport diverging at Hadley Junction and disappearing top left past the chimneys of Blockley's Brickworks.

Interior view of Blockley's No. 4 Works. Blockley's started making bricks in Hadley c. 1894 and, a century later, are the only surviving brickworks in the area.

Laying the foundation stone of New Hadley Methodist Chapel in 1932, this being a replacement for the United Methodist Free Church (see below).

Harold Holland (left), a miner, in conversation with Joe Holland, organist at New Hadley Methodist Chapel. The United Methodist Free Church, in the background, was demolished to enable Blockley's – whose chimneys are also visible – to extract clay from underneath.

Nos. 2, 4 and 6, Highfield Terrace, Hadley. Photographed shortly before demolition in 1963.

Waggon and horses outside the 'Bush Hotel' in High Street, Hadley a hundred years ago. Later replaced by another 'Bush', this too has now been demolished.

The rural surroundings of Hadley in times past allowed this lorry, operated by Clark & Smith, to collect milk churns from local farms for daily delivery to Birmingham where it is seen arriving at the Midland Counties Dairy in March 1933.

Nos. 12–22, High Street, Hadley and the 'Green Dragon' shortly before demolition in 1964.

Cars were something of a rarity in Trench when this picture was taken a few years after the First World War, but so were photographers, judging by the interest of the boy leaning out of the car window. The vehicle seems to have lost a headlight.

The Barley Mow, Hadley photographed for a Wrekin Brewery calendar, 1960.

View looking south up the Trench Inclined Plane, which closed to traffic in September 1921. The building to the right, at the top of the hill, was the Wombridge Pumping Engine House. It survived, minus chimney, as a local landmark until demolished on 27 December 1964.

There was still water in the canal until the 1960s. The 'Shropshire Arms' is visible on the left, and has since been re-named 'The Blue Pig'.

Looking north down the Trench Inclined Plane whilst it was still operating. The chimneys are mostly those of the Shropshire Iron Co.'s Trench Ironworks, producers of large quantities of wire.

A late 1940s view from a similar vantage point to the picture above. Trench Pool can still be seen on the right, though the inclined plane itself has become a footpath. The area has now been totally transformed by the construction of Queensway dual carriageway, descending towards the Trench Lock Interchange.

Trench Lock looking towards Wellington early this century. Not far from the present site of Poole's Garage.

Trench Crossing Station, looking south in the 1960s. Once a secluded spot, the location is now visible to the many motorists just south of the road from Trench Lock Interchange to Hortonwood Roundabout.

The canal lock from which Trench Lock derives its name, looking north in the direction of Hadley Park in 1948. All road traffic from Wellington and Hadley towards Donnington formerly passed over the narrow bridge at the foot of the lock.

Trench Methodist Chapel, on the corner of Trench Road and Church Road thirty years ago. The chapel bears a stone commemorating Lt-Col. James Patchett, a prominent local Wesleyan and manager of the Shropshire Iron Company's Trench Iron Works.

Much sub-standard housing was being demolished by local authorities before the coming of Telford New Town. This is the rear view of Forge Row, Hadley, prior to clearance in 1967.

Rear elevation of nos. 2, 4 and 6, Highfields Terrace, Hadley, pulled down in 1963.

Front elevation of Forge Row, Hadley. Many houses in this area were once occupied by workers at the Shropshire Iron Company, who employed several hundred men.

Outside lavatories at nos. 1–6 Victoria Road, Hadley.

The Duke of York, Trench, 35 years ago from a Wrekin Brewery calendar.

Six
Wrockwardine Wood and Wombridge

Beehive Corner, Wrockwardine Wood, a notorious traffic bottleneck in the 1960s. Only the building on the right survives near the junction of Lincoln Road and New Road, the latter now bisected by Wrockwardine Wood Way.

The stony track seen leading south westwards from the junction of Furnace Lane, Plough Road and Moss Road, Wrockwardine Wood towards the Cockshutt Piece follows the route of the Wrockwardine Wood Inclined Plane on the Shropshire Canal. Seen here in the 1960s, it is now crossed by Wrockwardine Wood Way, though the upper part remains as a footpath.

From the same camera position as the picture above, the photographer is now looking down the incline north eastwards towards Donnington. Wrockwardine Wood Central Methodist Hall can be seen in the distance.

Beehive Corner, Wrockwardine Wood, looking towards Wombridge. The flat-roofed building beyond the 'Hovis' sign survives on the truncated section of New Road to the south of Wrockwardine Wood Way, close to the junction with Lincoln Road.

Wrockwardine Wood Primitive Methodist Chapel has changed little since this photograph was taken thirty years ago, though the house obscured by the noticeboard has disappeared. Traffic now hurtles past on Wrockwardine Wood Way, just to the left. The carriageway leading to the church was laid out as a tribute to those from Wrockwardine Wood killed in the First World War.

This Victorian postcard of Wrockwardine Wood clearly shows the disused canal inclined plane rising from right to left with the Methodist Chapel on the skyline on the right. The tunnel underneath the incline is simply marked 'subway' on early large scale Ordnance Survey maps, though its original purpose is unclear.

Looking north from the slopes of Cockshutt Piece over Wrockwardine Wood in the 1960s. In the centre can be seen Holy Trinity Church, close to which, alongside the canal, stood Wrockwardine Wood glass works.

Bullock's Mill at Wrockwardine Wood, also known as Donnington Wood Mill, looking north west with the canal in the foreground. Wheat for this mill was the last traffic to use Trench Inclined Plane prior to its closure in 1921.

Unusual view of Wrockwardine Wood Mill taken from the churchyard of Holy Trinity Church looking south west. The tallest part of the mill bears a date stone from 1891, though there were buildings on the site from 1818.

Mrs Plant on her retirement as the Wombridge Crossing Keeper on 22 September 1966. Wombridge Way now crosses the railway just beyond the signal. Tickets to Birmingham are advertised on the crossing box at 11/6d (57½p) return or 7/6 (37½p) single.

A canal tunnel, which formed part of the Wombridge Canal, but the precise purpose of which was unknown, was discovered near Wombridge church during building work in 1965. It was subsequently backfilled.

The Valley Pool, with Wombridge church in the background three decades ago. Wombridge Way now crosses this area from right to left to meet Queensway at the Wombridge Interchange.

Class 3 of Wombridge National School. The school buildings were condemned in 1925, staff and pupils later moving to new premises at Hartshill.

Wombridge Road, looking towards Trench, during demolition of the railway bridge on the Wellington to Coalport line after closure in the early 1960s. Queensway was later constructed on the railway trackbed and, although there is a bridge across for pedestrians, the two halves of the road are now separated.

Path leading towards Oakengates from the Wombridge direction – a quiet walk before the building of Queensway dual carriageway.

Seven

Donnington and Donnington Wood

To Cyril
Best wishes

Sir Gordon Richards, the first jockey ever to be knighted, was born in Donnington Wood in 1905, the son of a Granville miner. In 1953, he won the Derby on 'Pinza'. This signed photograph was sent by him to Cyril Nicholls of the Lilleshall Company, where he had worked as a warehouse lad before becoming a jockey. The 'Champion Jockey' public house in Donnington and the 'Pinza Suite' at Oakengates Theatre are both named in his honour.

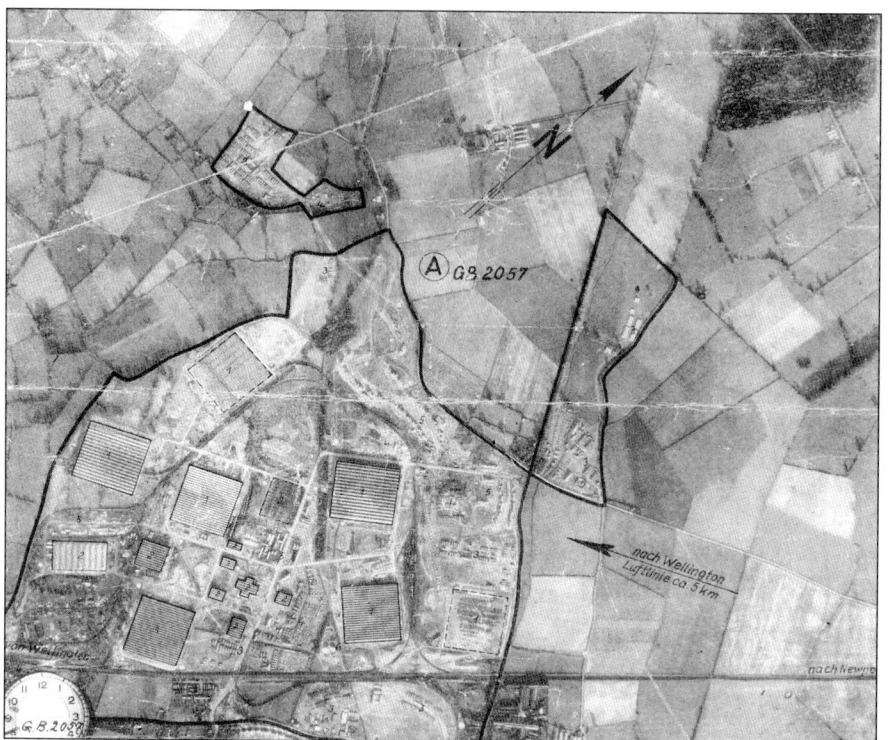

The establishment of the Central Ordnance Depot at Donnington in the 1930s was intended to lessen the risk of enemy bombing in the event of war, and huge quantities of stores were moved there from Woolwich Arsenal. This Luftwaffe map reveals that the Depot was known about by the Germans as a potential target.

Field House, Trench, which was demolished to make way for the Depot at Donnington.

A Duke of Sutherland cottage at Donnington, since dismantled and re-erected at Blists Hill Open Air Museum in the 1980s. The level crossing was on the Lilleshall Company railway network, and connected pits in the Donnington Wood area with the Wellington to Newport line.

A smart looking vehicle belonging to E. Hemmings & Son of Donnington. The load was being transported for Engineering Equipment Midlands Ltd of Wrockwardine Wood in the late 1950s.

The main offices of C. & W. Walker Ltd of Donnington, manufacturers of gasholders and similar equipment for the oil and chemical industries. A nineteenth century view looking from the Donnington railway station direction towards the Wellington to Newport road. The clock is now preserved on a nearby roundabout.

The Wellington to Newport railway alongside Walker's works, seen here 35 years ago, is now the route of the road to Newport and Stafford. The skeleton of the factory, which once extended over 18 acres and employed several hundred people, survived until a few years ago.

Interior of a section of the drawing office at Walker's taken from a 1950s brochure entitled *The Progress of C. & W. Walker Ltd.*

Interior of the steel department at Walker's showing one of the furnaces and a hydraulic press in the left foreground.

Steam winding engine at Granville colliery, manufactured by the Lilleshall Company.
Photographed in 1945.

Woodhouse Colliery, just north of Priorslee Hall, photographed at the turn of the century. The man in the foreground with his sleeves rolled up is Jack Fox. Over 700 people worked here in 1922, but production ceased in 1940.

General view of the pit head at Granville Colliery, north east of St Georges in 1944. At this time it was still owned by the Lilleshall Company, but was nationalised in 1947.

Winding drum at Granville Colliery in 1950. Although flat winding ropes had disappeared from the rest of the country many years earlier one was still in use at Granville at this time.

Underground photographs of local mines are comparatively rare. This 1938 picture shows the underground haulage road at Granville.

The modern headgear at Granville which was retained for some time after the last tub of coal was raised on 21 May 1979. Some of the redundant miners, who had numbered nearly 900 in 1967, transferred to pits in the Cannock area. The site is now a country park.

Part of the former Lilleshall Company railway system was taken over by the National Coal Board with coal mines acquired in 1947. Steam haulage survived as late as 1969, some of the coal going to Ironbridge Power Station via Wellington and Madeley Junction.

The Lilleshall Company's Donnington Wood Brickworks had a distinctive circular Hoffmann kiln. This post war view looking south westwards towards St Georges shows the clay pit, which had a cable-operated railway for hauling tubs of clay to the works.

A close-up of the sloping sides of the circular kilns 20 years later. The roof offered only a little protection from the elements.

Walkway leading from the top of the
kiln to one of the ancilliary buildings.
Note the chains preventing the walls
of the kiln from bulging with the heat.

Female labour was employed at
Donnington Wood. Mrs Wheeler, a
press operator, is seen at work in 1971,
and would have thought nothing of
hauling the trolley of unfired bricks
away when it was full.

View of Stephen's Water Engine Pit, Donnington Wood, showing the canal and a tub boat on the right. Though the pit closed by 1880, pumping continued to drain surrounding mines until 1928, the engine finally being scrapped in the 1930s.

The Lilleshall Company's Lodge Furnaces at Donnington Wood were highly regarded. The iron made there is described in Griffiths' *Guide to the Iron Trade*, published in 1873, as being without rival. This photograph was probably taken shortly after the furnaces were blown out in 1888.

Eight
Telford Town Centre

The modern face of Telford exemplified by prestige office blocks at the Town Centre.

St. Leonard's Church, Malinslee, just west of the Town Centre is now surrounded by housing, though its tower is visible from some distance to the south. Its main claim to fame is that it is thought to have been designed by Thomas Telford.

The Shropshire Association of Church Bellringers at St. Leonard's Church, Malinslee, in 1937 or 1938.

Pupils at the "Timber Yard" School, the precise location of which is not known. On the far left in the back row is Dr. Samuel Parkes Cadman (1864–1936) who later became a celebrated preacher in the United States.

Nineteen-fifties view from the south-east of Abbey Villas, Malinslee, which was demolished to make way for Telford Town Centre. The ruined Malinslee Chapel, dismantled for eventual re-erection in the Town Park, was beyond the hedge top right.

This is where Telford Town Centre now stands. Land in the foreground was once the site of Little Darklane Colliery, and Cartwright's Farm, Dark Lane, can be seen further north. Picture taken about 35 years ago.

Row of cottages which ran alongside the Wellington to Coalport railway line at Dark Lane, looking north towards Priorslee, as seen in about 1960. Demolished for the Town Centre and now the site of the Queensway, south of Hollinswood Interchange.

Looking west from Dark Lane Primitive Methodist Chapel at the second row of cottages at this settlement, built at right angles to those seen in the previous picture.

A close-up of Cartwright's Farm, Dark Lane, c. 1960. It can be seen top right in the photograph above. Demolished prior to the building of the Town Centre.

General view of Dark Lane looking north-east in about 1960. The Wellington to Coalport railway passed in front of the long row, and Malinslee Station was just to the right of the bridge seen in the right foreground.

A train storms westwards towards Wellington past Madeley Junction signalbox in September 1965, hauled by locomotive no. 6848 *Toddington Grange*. There is still a junction here, surrounded by the factories of Stafford Park, where coal trains turn off the main line on their way to Ironbridge Power Station.

A nineteen-sixties view of the ruinous California Brickworks, Dark Lane, which was situated on a restricted site, bounded on one side by the Shrewsbury–Birmingham railway, and on the other by the now closed Wellington–Coalport branch. Telford Central Station is now situated close to the site of Hollinswood Sidings, which can be seen in the background.

Priorslee Hall. Originally a private house, then head office of the Lilleshall Company, it became the headquarters of Dawley Telford Development Corporation in 1964 and is now part of the Priorslee campus of the University of Wolverhampton. Seen here in its original rural isolation, it is now surrounded by factories, houses and the M54 motorway.

Work on the M54 motorway in progress in the early 1980s. It was opened through to the M6 in 1983, though a short stretch south of Wellington had been completed as early as 1975.

Opencast mining occurred in various locations prior to building new roads and houses. This excavation is in the Old Park area. Malinslee House and the Town Park are discernible top left.

The success of modern Telford. View looking north eastwards across the Town Centre. Free parking and a brand new road network have succeeded in drawing shoppers and others from considerable distances outside the town.

Thomas Telford looks out on the town which bears his name. An inspired sculpture by Andre Wallace commissioned by Telford Development Corporation and unveiled in 1988.

Old Park survives as a fragment of the former community centred on an ironworks close to the site of the current Retail Park. Centenary celebrations are announced for April 1953 on the noticeboard outside Hilltop Methodist Church.

A donkey and cart feature in the Old Park carnival at an unspecified date early this century.

Nine
Around the Wrekin

The Forest Glen, at the foot of the Wrekin, was built by Henry William Pointon in 1889, primarily to provide refreshments and a comfort stop for those climbing the hill. It later became the venue for functions of all kinds.

Joe Pointon pours out German wine for Billy Griffiths, Herbert Farnall, Lu Etchells, Bill Boffey, Harry Pointon and friends from Stoke in front of the Forest Glen more than 70 years ago.

An inter-war picture of a car outing with the Wrekin in the background. Mr E. Brown is on the right in the back seat with Mrs B. Bagley and Mrs Brown (standing to the right of the car).

The Wrekin has been a subject for photographers ever since the camera was invented. This very early photo, with a child posing in the foreground, is captioned "The Wrekin from Leighton".

The Forest Glen as many thousands will remember it. This unidentified function was held there in 1959. The building was re-erected at Blists Hill Open Air Museum in 1994.

Acknowledgements

The compilers would like to record special thanks to Terry Blud, Denis Fry, Ken Jones and Barrie Trinder for help with this volume, and to David Houlston and Marlene Taylor of D.J. Houlston Photography for providing such an excellent service to the Museum over many years. The Social History Group of the Friends of the Ironbridge Gorge Museum deserves special mention, currently active members not already named being Fred Brian, Jim Cooper, Ruth Crofts, Sheila and Harold Grice, Terry Howells, and Cath and Jack Marshall. Thanks must also go to all participants, both living and deceased, in the Friends Oral History Programme, and their relatives, who have proved such a marvellous source of unique photographs. Whilst it is not possible to credit every single picture (indeed, some donors have requested anonymity) thanks go to Mrs Allan, Brian and Trevor Bagley, Maureen Bond, Ivor Brown, C.E.G. Budd, Mr Bullock, Graham Daniels, Betty Duddell, Margaret Duvaston, Ken and Margaret Fowler, Mr and Mrs Garbett, Michael Hale, Mrs Jones, Dorinda Jones, T. Langford, Mrs Lawrence, Geoffrey Lewis, Miss M.E. McCrea, John Marcham, Ron Miles, Cyril Nicholls, F. Ogden, Mary Onions, Angela Pearson, Les Pugh, Eustace Rogers, Nigel Rowe, Shropshire Star Newspapers, Janet Slack, George Teece, Emyr Thomas, Neville Upton, Wendy Waterson, Mrs K. Watling and Geoff Wheeldon. Colleagues at the Ironbridge Gorge Museum to be thanked for their help and forebearance include Marilyn Higson, Dianna Stiff and volunteer Joyce Hiscox. Joanne Smith has been invaluable, not only for years of conscientiously cataloguing the Museum's pictorial collection, but also for typing and checking captions for this book. Glen Lawes and Peter Jennings are also thanked for backing the project enthusiastically from the outset.